TOYS

Around the World

by Joanna Brundle

©2016
Book Life
King's Lynn
Norfolk PE30 4LS

ISBN: 978-1-910512-88-3

All rights reserved
Printed in Spain

Written by:
Joanna Brundle

Designed by:
Natalie Carr

A catalogue record for this book
is available from the British Library.

CONTENTS

You can find the blue words in this book in the Glossary on page 24.

Where in the WORLD?

COUNTRIES:

1. Australia
2. China
3. Japan
4. India
5. Russia
6. France
7. Norway
8. England
9. Wales
10. Scotland
11. Belgium
12. Germany
13. Spain
14. Ivory Coast
15. Canada
16. USA
17. Peru
18. Austria
19. Kenya
20. Guatemala
21. Ethiopia

Look at this map to find the countries we are going to read about.

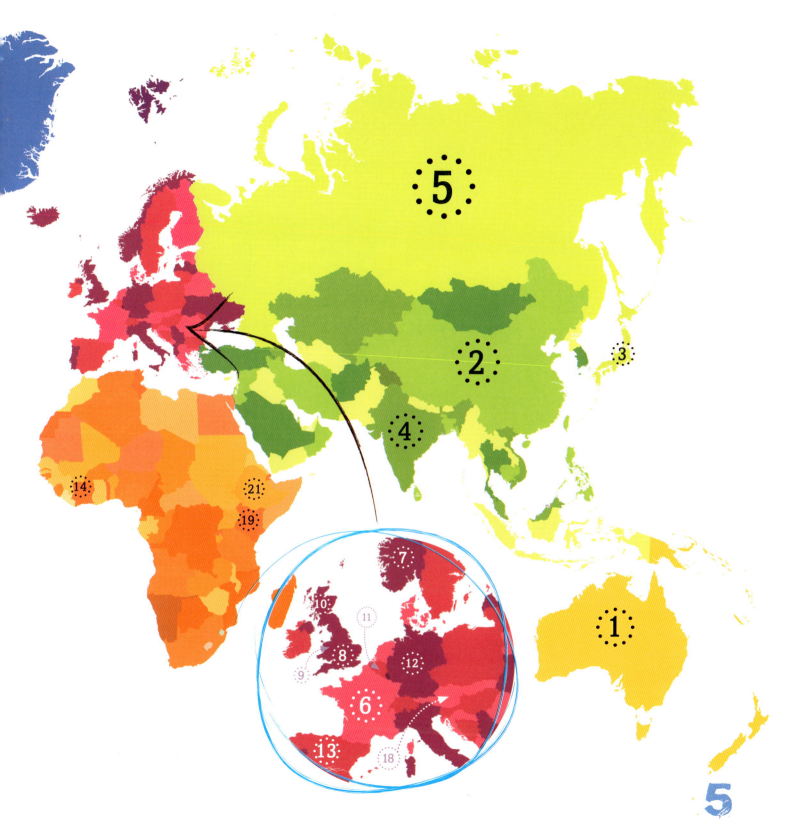

5

TOYS and the Natural WORLD

Conkers is played in England.

In African countries, skipping ropes are made of dried plant stems which have been twisted together. Children in Ivory Coast collect pebbles to play a game called Mancala.

To win a game of Mancala, you have to capture more stones than the other player. You win stones by dropping them into an empty space on the board.

Soft toys that look like animals are popular all around the world. Do you have a koala or kangaroo from Australia, or a panda from China?

Australia

China

SUN and SNOW

Climate affects how children play. In hot, dry countries like Spain, toys for the beach and swimming pool are popular.

In snowy countries like Norway and Canada, children ski, ice skate and play with sledges and **snow boards.**

Ice Skating

Sledging Fun!

9

DOLLS

Worry Doll

Russian dolls, like the ones on the front cover, are painted in bright colours and fit inside one another. Children in Guatemala tell their dolls their worries. They put the dolls under their pillow and in the morning, the worry has gone!

Can you see the hand-made beads on these African rag dolls?

Many countries have a national costume. Dolls wearing these outfits are made all round the world.

These national costumes are from Russia, China and The Netherlands.

JAPAN and CHINA

In Japan, a cup and ball game called Kendama is popular. Children also like Uta Garuta (a card game) and Kokeshi dolls. They are carved from wood.

Kendama Set

Kokeshi Doll

12

Kite flying has been popular in China for thousands of years. Children also like playing Tangram, which is a puzzle.

Chinese Tangram

Kite flying is fun!

EUROPE

Children playing Petanque on the beach.

A traditional Petanque set

In France, a favourite toy is a stuffed giraffe called Sophie. French children also play Petanque, which is like bowls.

In The Netherlands, children play Sjoelbak. They have to push thirty discs through four small archways as fast as they can. It is also played in Germany and Belgium.

A Sjoelbak set

RUSSIA and INDIA

Russian children like to play with a mosaics set called Mozaika. They make pictures by putting coloured pegs in holes.

Pegs for Mozaika

Look at the pattern this girl has made. What picture would you make?

In India, a game similar to pool is played. It is called Carrom. Children also play a board game called Goats and Tigers. Their tigers have to capture the other players' goats.

A family playing Carrom

Carrom pieces

A pool table

AFRICA

Children in Ethiopia playing with a hoop and stick.

In Kenya, children play with model cars and bicycles made of wire, called Galimoto. Children sometimes make the models themselves. They use sticks and stalks of corn too.

In Zimbabwe, children play Kudoda. They throw a pebble and have to pick up as many others as they can before the pebble hits the floor.

In England, we call this game Jacks.

USA

In the USA, an old-fashioned toy called Lincoln Logs is still popular. Children make models of castles, forts and pirate ships from small logs that fit together.

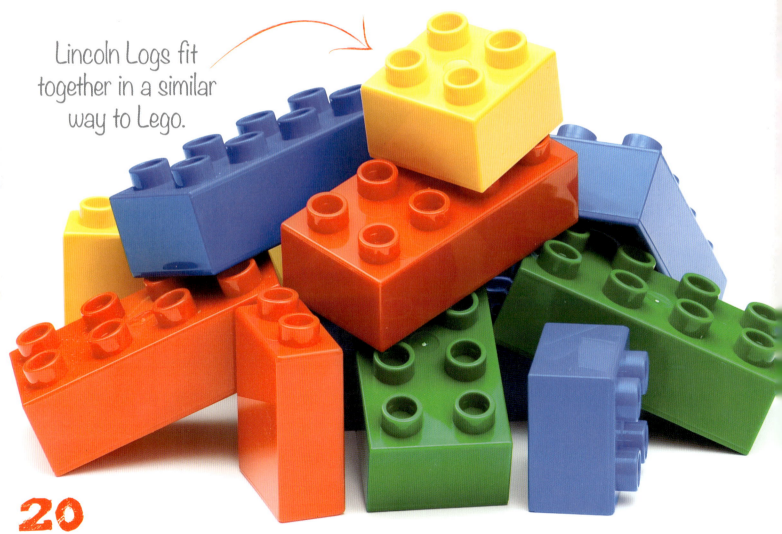

Lincoln Logs fit together in a similar way to Lego.

SAME BUT DIFFERENT

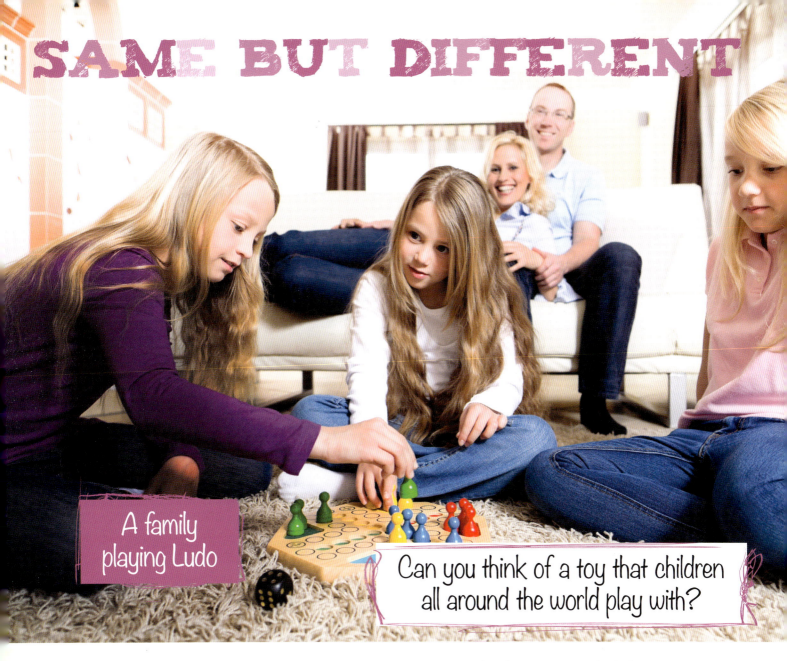

A family playing Ludo

Can you think of a toy that children all around the world play with?

Some toys are the same all around the world but look different or have different names. Ludo is called "Sorry" in Japan. In Austria, it is called "Don't be upset".

FUN FACTS

1 The largest Russian doll has fifty-one pieces and is fifty-four centimetres tall.

2 Four out of five toys are made in China.

3 Rapunzel Barbie was sold in fifty-nine countries on her **launch day**.

4 You can play computer games with other children all around the world.

23

GLOSSARY

CLIMATE
The average weather in any country

LAUNCH DAY
The first day an item is sold

NATIONAL COSTUME
A traditional style of dress for a country

OLD-FASHIONED
Not modern

SNOW BOARDS
Boards you stand on to glide over snow